D0641129

Other giftbooks by Helen Exley:

Words of Joy

Words on Hope

Thoughts on... Being Happy

The Precious Present

Words on Calm

Words on Beauty

Published simultaneously in 1998 by Helen Exley Giftbook
in Great Britain and Helen Exley Giftbooks LLC in the US

Copyright © Helen Exley 1998

PAM BROWN: published with permission © Helen
Exley 1998

The moral right of the author has been asserted.

12 11 10 9

ISBN 1-86187-054-X

Quotations selected by Helen Exley.

Illustrated by Angela Kerr.

Printed in China.

**Helen Exley Giftbooks, 16 Chalk Hill, Watford,
Herts WD19 4BG, UK.
Helen Exley Giftbooks LLC, 185 Main Street,
Spencer, MA 01562, USA.**
www.helenexleygiftbooks.com

SEIZE THE DAY!
Enjoy the moment

A HELEN EXLEY
GIFTBOOK

≣EXLEY

Nothing is worth more than this day.

JOHANN WOLFGANG VON GOETHE

If I had my life to live over...
I would perhaps have more
actual troubles,
But I'd have fewer
imaginary ones.

NADINE STAIR

It is so hard for us little human beings to accept this deal that we get. It's really crazy, isn't it? We get to live, then we have to die. What we put into every moment is all we have....

GILDA RADNOR

Stars over snow,
And in the west a planet swinging
below a star –
Look for a lovely thing and you
will find it,
It is not far – It never will be far.

SARA TEASDALE, "NIGHT"

Carpe diem, quam minimum
credula a postero.
Seize the day, and put the least
possible trust in tomorrow.

HORACE

You don't get to choose how you're going to die. Or when. You can only decide how you're going to live. Now.

JOAN BAEZ, FROM "DAYBREAK"

Eternity is not something that begins after you are dead. It is going on all the time. We are in it now.

CHARLOTTE PERKINS GILMAN

Give us grace, O God, to dare to do the deed which we well know cries to be done. Let us not hesitate because of ease, or the words of [people]'s mouths, or our own lives.

W.E.B. DU BOIS

When any one of us says: "I will live tomorrow," he indulges in a dangerous fantasy about living. The life that the dawn brings us is the only life we have.

VIMALA THAKAR

Accept the pain,
cherish the joy,
resolve the regrets;
then can come
the best of
benedictions – "If
I had my life to do
over, I'd do it all
the same."

JOAN MCINTOSH

A life of reaction is a life of slavery, intellectually and spiritually. One must fight for a life of action, not reaction.

RITA MAE BROWN

*L*ife engenders life.
Energy creates energy.
It is by spending
oneself that
one becomes rich.

SARAH BERNHARDT

For every person who has ever lived there has come, at last, a spring he will never see. Glory then in the springs that are yours.

PAM BROWN

I choose to inhabit my days, to

allow my living

to open me, to make me less

afraid, more accessible, to

loosen my heart until it becomes

a wing, a torch, a promise.

DAWNA MARKOVA

*I will not be just a tourist
in the world of images,
just watching images
passing by which I cannot
live in, make love to,
possess as permanent
sources of joy and ecstasy.*

ANAÏS NIN

*I had not loved enough.
I'd been busy, busy, so
busy, preparing for life,
while life floated by me,
quiet and swift as a
regatta.*

LORENE CARY

Enjoy the blessings

of the day... and the

evils bear patiently;

for this day only is ours:

we are dead to yesterday,

and not born to tomorrow.

JEREMY TAYLOR

*Life
itself
is
the
proper
binge.*

JULIA CHILD

And *whatsoever* *you do,* *do it* *heartily.*

COLOSSIANS 3:23

I wish I knew what people meant when they say they find "emptiness" in this wonderful adventure of living, which seems to me to pile up its glories like an horizon-wide sunset as the light declines.

EDITH WHARTON

What worth has beauty, if it is not seen?

ITALIAN PROVERB

*Every year I live
I am more convinced
that the waste of life lies in
the love we have not given,
the powers we
have not used, the
selfish prudence that
will risk nothing....*

MARY CHOLMONDELEY

... if you really and sincerely and passionately want to do something (and wholeheartedly, with the whole of your sincerest self) it is by doing that that you will be most useful, will be giving the most, will be of most individual value.

ANNE MORROW LINDBERGH

I want to live only for ecstasy. Small doses, moderate loves, all half-shades, leave me cold. I like extravagance. Letters which give the postman a stiff back to carry, books which overflow from their covers, sexuality which bursts the thermometers.

ANAÏS NIN

You can have anything you want if you want it desperately enough. You must want it with an exuberance that erupts through the skin and joins the energy that created the world.

It's only when we truly know and understand that we have a limited time on earth – and that we have no way of knowing when our time is up that we will begin to live each day to the fullest, as if it was the only one we had.

ELISABETH KÜBLER-ROSS

Don't evaluate your life in terms of achievements, trivial or monumental, along the way ... Instead, wake up and appreciate everything you encounter along the path. Enjoy the flowers that are there for your pleasure. Tune in to the sunrise, the little children, the laughter, the rain, and the birds. Drink it all in ... there is no way to happiness; happiness is the way.

DR WAYNE W. DYER

Gather ye rosebuds while ye may,
Old time is still a-flying:
And this same flower that smiles today
Tomorrow will be dying.

Sometimes I would almost
rather have people take away
years of my life than take away
a moment.

PEARL BAILEY

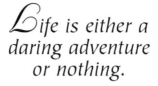

Life is either a
daring adventure
or nothing.

HELEN KELLER

I believe that life should
be lived so vividly and so
intensely that thoughts of
another life, or of a longer
life, are not necessary.

MARJORY STONEMAN DOUGLAS

A new life begins for us
with every second. Let us
go forward joyously to
meet it. We must press on,
whether we will or no,
and we shall walk better with
our eyes before us
than with them ever cast
behind.

JEROME K. JEROME

It is time for every one of us to roll up our sleeves and put ourselves at the top of our commitment list.

MARIAN WRIGHT EDELMAN

Anyone can carry his burden, however hard, until nightfall. Anyone can do his work, however hard, for one day. Anyone can live sweetly, patiently, lovingly, purely, till the sun goes down. And this is all that life really means.

ROBERT LOUIS STEVENSON

With life I am on the
attack, restlessly ferreting
out each pleasure, foraging
for answers, wringing from
it even the pain.
I ransack life, hunt it down.

MARITA GOLDEN

*B*ut warm, eager,
living life – to be
rooted in life –
to learn, to desire to
know, to feel, to think,
to act. That is what
I want. And nothing
else. That is what
I must try for.

KATHERINE MANSFIELD

If the engine whistles, let it whistle till it is hoarse for its pains. If the bell rings, why should we run? Time is but the stream I go a-fishing in.

HENRY DAVID THOREAU

It is time to come to your senses. You are to live and to learn to laugh. You are to learn to listen to the cursed radio music of life and to reverence the spirit behind it and to laugh at its distortions. So there you are. More will not be asked of you.

HERMANN HESSE
(1877-1962)

That it will never come again is what makes life so sweet.

EMILY DICKINSON

*To see a World in a Grain of Sand
And a Heaven in a Wild Flower,
Hold infinity in the palm of your hand
and Eternity in an hour.*

WILLIAM BLAKE

Enjoy the little things,
for one day you may
look back and discover
they were the big things.

AUTHOR UNKNOWN

The best things are nearest:
breath in your nostrils, light in
your eyes, flowers at your feet,
duties at your hand, the path
of Right just before you. Do
not grasp at the stars, but do
life's plain common work as it
comes, certain that daily duties
and daily bread are the
sweetest things in life.

ROBERT LOUIS STEVENSON

To fill the hour –

that is happiness; to fill

the hour, and leave no

crevice for a repentance

or an approval.

RALPH WALDO EMERSON

Between the house and
the store there are little
pockets of happiness.
A bird, a garden, a friend's
greeting, a child's smile,
a cat in the sunshine
needing a stroke.
Recognize them or
ignore them. It's always
up to you.

PAM BROWN

To be reborn hourly and daily in this life, we need to die – to give of ourselves wholly to the demands of the moment, so that we utterly "disappear". Thoughts of past, present, or future, of life and death, of this world and the next, are transcended in the superabundance of the now. Time and timelessness *coalesce: this is the moment of eternity. Thus our every act is a matter either of giving life or taking it away. If we perform each act with total absorption, we give life to our life. If we do things half-heartedly, we kill that life.*

PHILIP KAPLEAU

*I struggle to live for the
beauty of a pansy
for a little black baby's song
for my lover's laugh
I struggle for the blaze of
pink across the evening sky
for some bar-b-cue ribs
I struggle for life and the
pursuit of its happiness
I struggle to fill my house
with joy*

STEPHANIE BYRD

There is no perfect time to get away... just do it!

ANONYMOUS

Get on with living and loving. You don't have forever.

LEO F. BUSCAGLIA

Everything is unique, nothing happens more than once in a lifetime. The physical pleasure which a certain woman gave you at a certain moment, the exquisite dish which you ate on a certain day – you will never meet either again. Nothing is repeated, and everything is unparalleled.

EDMOND AND JULES
GONCOURT

Since life is short and the world is wide, the sooner you start exploring it the better. Soon enough the time will come when you are too tired to move farther than the terrace of the best hotel. Go now.

SIMON RAVEN

The follies which a person regrets the most in his life, are those which he didn't commit when he had the opportunity.

HELEN ROWLAND

*We all grow up at last
and lose that first sharp
vision of the world. We
miss dew sparkle, leaf
shadow, spider scuttle,
puddle shine. We waste time
on worry. And we find the
days sweep by, each
blurred, each like the other.*

PAM BROWN

We are here so short
a while. Savour the
moment as it passes.
This is your shining
hour - all the glory
of the universe is
yours.

PAM BROWN

Seize every minute
Of your time.
The days fly by;
Ere long you too
Will grow old.

If you believe me not,
See there, in the courtyard,
How the frost
Glitters white and cold
and cruel
On the grass
That once was green.

TZU YEH

It is awesome to think that everything is one's own, at least for the brief space of a life – which is why I have always the sense I must hurry to get things done, that there is hardly any time at all for a man to impress his quality and passion upon a world which will continue after him, as unconcerned as it was when it preceded him.

GORE VIDAL

Spend all you have for loveliness,
Buy it and never count the cost;
For one white singing hour of peace
Count many a year of strife well lost,
And for a breath of ecstasy
Give all that you have been, or could be.

SARA TEASDALE

Let us spend one day as deliberately as nature, and not be thrown off the track by every nutshell and mosquito's wing that falls on the rails. Let us rise early and fast, or break fast, gently and without perturbation; let company come and let company go, let the bells ring and the children cry.

HENRY DAVID THOREAU

*L*ife is a succession

of moments.

To live each one is

to succeed.

CORITA KENT

I have learned to live

each day as it comes

and not to borrow

trouble by dreading

tomorrow.

DOROTHY DIX

People do not live nowadays – they get about ten percent out of life.

ISADORA DUNCAN

... we live in the past or in the future; we are continually expecting the coming of some special moment when our life will unfold itself in its full significance. And we do not notice that life is flowing like water through our fingers.

FATHER ALEXANDER
ELCHANINOV

Life was meant to be lived and curiosity must be kept alive. One must never, for whatever reason, turn one's back on life.

ELEANOR ROOSEVELT

*People
for the
sake of
getting
a living
forget
to live.*

MARGARET FULLER

*Flow with whatever
may happen and let
your mind be free. Stay
centered by accepting
whatever you are doing.
This is the ultimate.*

CHUANG TSU

I expect to pass through life but once. If therefore, there be any kindness I can show, or any good thing I can do to any fellow being, let me do it now, and not defer or neglect it, as I shall not pass this way again.

WILLIAM PENN

Make hay while the sun shines.

PROVERB

Write it on your heart that every day is the best day in the year.

RALPH WALDO EMERSON

Each day that I live I say to myself: the visible world is mine, use it, change it, but be quick, for the night comes all too fast and nothing is ever entirely finished, nothing.

GORE VIDAL

The biggest sin is sitting on your ass.

FLORYNCE KENNEDY

I will not die an unlived life.
I will not live in fear
of falling or catching fire.

DAWNA MARKOVA

They are committing murder who merely live.

MAY SARTON

Security is when everything is settled, when nothing can happen to you; security is the denial of life.

GERMAINE GREER

How can you hesitate? Risk! Risk anything! Care no more for the opinion of others, for those voices. Do the hardest thing on earth for you. Act for yourself. Face the truth.

KATHERINE MANSFIELD

*Everyone should have
a chance at a
breathtaking piece of
folly at least
once in his life.*

ELIZABETH TAYLOR

I don't want to get
to the end of my life
and find that I lived
just the length of it.
I want to have lived
the width of it as
well.

DIANE ACKERMAN

*Life is in the here
and now, not in the
there and afterwards.
The day, with all
the travail and joy
that it brings to our
doorstep, is the
expression of
eternal life. Either we
meet it, we live it –
or we miss it.*

VIMALA THAKAR

Make voyages.
Attempt them.
That's all
there is.

ELAINE DUNDY

Do not linger to gather flowers to keep them, but walk on, for flowers will keep themselves blooming all your way.

RABINDRANATH TAGORE

*Never say –
"One day I'll
venture...". The
moment is now.*

PAM BROWN

When I'm old I'm never going to say, "I didn't do this" or, "I regret that." I'm going to say, "I don't regret a damn thing. I came, I went, and I did it all."

KIM BASINGER